PROFILING THE LEFT

by

JOSHUA VAN ASAKINDA

ISBN-13: 978-1721628421
ISBN-10: 1721628428

For a dead old German, and a dead old Russian,
who taught me how to hunt down lies.

Table of Contents

Author's Introduction

This is what is known as a polemic.

It is an attack, but not against any particular individual; rather, it is directed against a vast network of ideas that has slowly but surely eaten away at the fabric of society for generations now, which I refer to loosely as *post-modernism.* My hope is that this book will incite a reaction; that seems the best way to disseminate an idea these days. Fortunately, the character of the enemy is almost entirely *reactionary:* He is hardly able *not to* respond; in fact, he is incapable of doing otherwise. This is because his worldview is grounded in *condemnation.* It only *negates;* it never *creates.*

Historically speaking, post-modernism is the answer to the question of modernism, though the two are distinct philosophical movements. Modernism arose in the late 1800s and held sway through the boom of the American economy after World War II. During this time, modernists began wondering whether or not the old order- "God," "spirit," "religion," "democracy," "capitalism"- were even tenable anymore. But it was not until the advent of *post*-modernism that the question was answered: "All are wanting, so off with its head!" So in a sense, *modernism* was characterized by a kind of back-looking skepticism while *post*-modernism was and continues to be characterized by a kind of forward-looking nihilism.

Modernism gave birth to post-modernism, clearly, but the solutions proposed by post-modernists are hardly the only possible solutions to the problems of modernism. It is entirely valid to wonder, "How can society move forward without forgetting the past, and *if* we are to move forward, is it possible to do so *without* forgetting the past?" However, it is not entirely valid to therefore assert as the post-modernists do, "No, there is no moving forward *unless* we forget the past, and in fact, *all* of the past must be forgotten *in order* to move forward *at all.*" This is a *non sequitor.*

The fact that a solution is *unknown* does not render it *impossible.*

Clearly, we could have approached this process of reevaluation with a scalpel; post-modernism went with the hammer. "All of it must burn!" But why should *all of it* burn? There is no clear reason why *all of it* should burn. It is almost as though it was not reason at all that spoke through their answer, but something *deceitful, questionable, pathological...*

The early post-modernists argued that religion was becoming more secularized, cultures were becoming less isolated, traditional social structures were breaking down, and that *therefore,* the old order was irrelevant; the industrialization of the world demanded the creation of new systems. And so post-modernism became particularly common among socialists and communists who were already looking forward to the destruction of the old order as a necessary prerequisite for establishing global Marxism. Wherever one looked, one found *ennui;* this mass contempt for the old order was at least in part due to the socio-psychological trauma caused by the horrific atrocities committed by totalitarian regimes during and following two World Wars, which resulted in a general revulsion towards grand ideologies of any kind. Yet at the same time, we had conquered fascism; we had split the atom; we had blazed a trail of new ideas pregnant with new possibilities.

Wherever we see that Marxism held sway, the masses grew to worship whatever was *new* merely because it was *not* old, and any tradition, no matter how ancient or admired, was condemned outright. The downstream consequences of this would prove to be catastrophic; the baby had been thrown out with the bathwater, but few knew it. Some in the West were rightly alarmed by this course of events, of course, but they stood in the minority. And as we learn from studying history, it is too often the case that, according to Henrik Ibsen, "The majority has *might,* more's the pity, but *right* it has not. *Right-* are I and a few others."

We might imagine that such a scenario would result in the revitalization of the classical tradition across the European-American world, but we would be disappointed. Sadly, the West doubled down on all its favorite "-isms"- "materialism," "corporatism," "consumerism," "globalism," "deconstructionism," etc. Before long, "the Almighty Dollar" had taken the place of faith, family, and fatherland as the entire European-American world began rushing headlong into raw, soulless self-engorgement. Nothing much mattered but money, and what pleasures money could buy; predictably, the pursuit of more meaningful goals became *passé.* And so the West became ground zero for our current cult of self-gratification.

The early adherents to the post-modern movement were Marxists almost without exception, and therefore had long anticipated the passing away of the *bourgeoisie.* For this reason, they saw in post-modernism a kindred spirit, and the two movements began to rapidly merge, especially in academic circles. Marxists saw rampant materialism not as the clarion call to return to the wrongly-condemned classical tradition but rather as the death knell of a fraudulent worldview- the old order itself- that to their minds never should have existed in the first place. Gradually, that animosity hastened the disintegration of the classical tradition: Modernism was its sickness; post-modernism ensured its final, shuddering breath.

Post-modernism is today closely related to- although not quite synonymous with- liberalism, especially among progressives, who are *quintessential* post-modernists. It is difficult to even imagine present-day liberalism without the admixture of Marxism and post-modernism. Once, liberalism was allied to the classical tradition; now, it stands in direct contra-distinction to it. For while present-day liberals are steeped in post-modernism, post-modernists are not liberals in the philosophical sense. Historically, liberalism was synonymous with neo-classicism up until very recently; the Founding Fathers are correctly described as *classical liberals,* though few today would refer to the Founding Fathers as liberals of any kind. Similarly, the worldview of John F. Kennedy- a recent advocate of *pre-progressive* liberalism-, now looks remarkably like republicanism.

This is why so many democrats and independents abandoned the DNC for the RNC from 2016-2024: Donald Trump, Elon Musk, Joe Rogan, Tulsi Gabbard, Robert F. Kennedy, Jr., etc. And let us not forget that Ronald Reagan himself was once a disaffected democrat. The term liberalism had exchanged its original *philosophical* meaning for a new, post-modernist *political* meaning. Consequently, old school liberals quit their respective parties over the course of generations, and so conservatism grew as a result, not because it had anything in the way of *new* ideas but merely because it did not wish to destroy all the *old* ideas.

For this reason, we should clarify that when we refer to *liberalism* in this book, we are referring to liberalism in the sense in which it is used today- that is, in the progressive, neo-Marxist sense-, and *not* in its early, correct philosophical sense. Not everyone identified with the *political* left is *philosophically* left, just as not everyone identified with the *political* right is *philosophically* right. Furthermore, not every person on the left is necessarily left on *every* subject, just as not every person on the right is necessarily right on *every* subject. We are not monoliths; we are not uni-dimensional individuals. People are complicated. Sometimes we adopt ideas piecemeal, and often discover upon inspection that clear and well-defined categories break down. Savvy politicians know this, and so tend to speak to the middle; less savvy politicians prefer to message only to their base. Unfortunately, the latter outnumber the former, and so the old pendulum of political divisiveness continues to swing forever…

The purpose of this book is not to attack any particular *political party* but rather to show that there is a distinct *psychological pattern* shared by certain types of radicals and reactionaries on either side of the political aisle. At this moment, they tend to gravitate to the left, thus the title of this book. But they could one day begin gravitating to the right, and so what this book is describing in some sense applies regardless of political affiliation. The fact that we are applying these principles to the left is a point *of history* more so than a point *in principle.*

The lukewarm Protestant who votes Republican may very well be a liberal at heart; conversely, the union Catholic who votes Democrat may very well be a cultural traditionalist. We have often assumed that Latinos are left-leaning in spite of the fact that Latinos tend to be Catholic, pro-life, and family-oriented. This applies equally well to Asian and Jewish communities, which are generally quite conservative regardless of their voting behaviors. So we must be careful not to draw the boundaries of our categories too sharply, for while politics does tend to make people stupid, individuals are complex, and often hold complex (and even self-contradictory) systems of beliefs.

Still, general tendencies do exist, and these tendencies are often pronounced. Generalizations are regrettable, but they are a regrettable necessity; expediency demands their use unless we are willing to discuss individually each and every one of the seven billion plus human beings living in the world today. And so generally speaking and in terms of his voting behavior, the modern political liberal has abandoned liberalism for post-modernism. But what *exactly* is the meaning of post-modernism?

A quick lesson in the history of western philosophy may be in order: The European classical tradition, which began around the time of Socrates and informed the development of European-American culture well into the late 20th century, was founded upon the assertion that there *are* absolutes, universals that are not only *knowable* but that *ought to be discovered.* Knowing these truths was wisdom (σοφία, or *sophia*), which was itself the goal; in fact, the word *philosophy* (φίλοσοφία, or *philosophia*) means literally in Greek, "love of wisdom." So the pursuit of truth stood foremost among moral imperatives, and rightly so. For the classicist, *sans* truth, there is nothing.

And for reasons that stand outside the scope of this book, this prime imperative towards wisdom has been- at least historically- rooted in religion. At the heart of every religion, we see shared principles: We are made in the *imago dei* ("image of God"); *therefore,* we are free-willed because God is free-willed; *therefore,* if we are free to will or not to will, then we are *fully responsible* for ourselves. And so the pursuit of wisdom goes hand in hand with personal responsibility for *if* we are fully responsible for ourselves, *then* it would seem reasonable to pursue wisdom as much as humanly possible. Such a pursuit would be right and godly in two senses: First, it would be cultivating the divine wisdom within ourselves; second, it would allow us to live better, more fulfilling lives.

And the whole world was built upon this idea.

But what might we find when science comes along and makes us wonder if we are *not* free, if we are really nothing more than atoms, if we are really nothing more than glorified dominoes falling one by one? What we *may* find is a great deal of resentment by those at the bottom of the social hierarchy- towards God, towards religion, towards government, towards all the structures of civilization. Essentially, this rift marks the historical axis around which everything in western society rotates: Since that point, western society has been divided against itself, with half defending the old order against the attacks (some justified, some not so much) of the other half, who imagine some new, better, perfected utopia.

Modernism, as we have said, asked the question, "Is the old order relevant today?" And in and of itself, that is a fine question to ask; in fact, questions such as this are the lifeblood of civilization. However, the response among post-modernists has been *purely reactionary:* "No, it is all rotten! Raze it to the ground, damn the consequences…"

What we ended up with was relativism rooted in the need to constantly negate whatever is old- including truth, logic, religion, orthodoxy, philosophy, etc. "Truth," according to Napoleon, "is a lie agreed upon." Post-modernists agree, but without Napoleon's sense of irony, for the sentiment has become entirely representative of post-modernist doctrine- that "truth" merely serves a purpose. Universals are *unnecessary,* argue the post-modernists, and not *only* unnecessary; they- like the entirety of the old order- are actually "systems of oppression," and they ought therefore to be abolished.

Post-modernism has effectively co-opted liberalism; now the tail wags the dog. Little of classical liberalism exists on the left today because the limiting principles of truth, reason, religion, etc. have been abandoned. Without limiting principles, worldviews- however sophisticated- go quite quickly off the rails because like any other creation of the human being, they are subject to the whim of human passion, whether that whim be lust, hatred, delusion (the Three Poisons of Buddhism), or whatever.

So what, exactly, did we lose?

Well, let us define our terms. For our purposes, the classical tradition, which has been under attack by post-modernists for a century and a half now, may be defined as 1. the belief that man ought to be at liberty, but within boundaries constrained by truth, and only in order that he should flourish according to that very same truth; 2. that *outer* liberty is predicated upon *inner* dignity; and 3. that this dignity is the consequence of *self-discipline, ethical behavior,* and *the mastery of the various passions.* Take special note of the fact that insofar as classicism is concerned, freedom is *not* a meaning in and of itself; freedom is bounded by a higher calling, specifically the pursuit of *eudaimonia* (εὐδαιμονία)- "noble-spiritedness" or the flourishing of the human being- via *arete* (ἀρετή)- excellence, and specifically of the kind of excellence that pertains to virtue, or as the Greeks called it, "the good." Classicism, therefore, is deeply moral in character, and cannot be otherwise. Furthermore, it is universalist in orientation; it applies to everyone equally. Truth, after all, is the same no matter whether one is a philosopher or a barbarian, and this universality provides a measure by which to gauge the strength and sophistication of either an individual or an organization, regardless of their sex, race, creed, etc.

Reverence for truth necessarily results in logical restrictions upon *all* individuals regardless of social position, so that the actions of anyone no matter how powerful could theoretically be brought into question by anyone no matter how powerless. And so from the point of view of politics in its *amoral* sense, the classical tradition is *dangerous*. For men who possess power- or worse, for men who thirst for power that they have never possessed- are not fond of the marketplace of ideas. The power-mad thrive, after all, not under conditions of *reason* but under conditions of *passion;* they are experts in *the exploitation of desire* (turn on literally any talking-head political discussion for proof of this). And so it should come as no surprise that philosophers- "lovers of wisdom"- have forever been the enemies of social, personal, and political tyranny (insofar as these are *actual* rather than *imagined*- an important distinction). Consequently, classicism is a stumbling block for those who wish either for their desires or for the desires of their subjects (i.e. voters) to remain unchecked.

We should not be surprised that even Socrates was put to death by the powerful of Athens, and for "corrupting the youth." But how *exactly* had Socrates corrupted the youth? Merely by teaching a very dangerous idea- that *even the gods must obey what is right.* However, in so doing, he had checked the powerful as well, for *if the will of the gods* can be checked, *then the will of their representatives* can be likewise checked.

And so, the hemlock…

There are certain kinds of people that find themselves attracted to positions of power; they are not often fond of boundaries. This is because that type of person is oftentimes incapable of discipline, and thus enslaved to his own passions. Generally, the burning desire for *external* control is merely a counterbalance to the instability that follows from a lack of *internal* control; it is an attempt at *ordering reality.* He *wants* control *because* he cannot control himself. But the stable personality does not require external control; he is self-sufficient. And this applies equally well to criminals in prison as to psychopaths in positions of power, whether of Hollywood, Wall Street, or Washington, D.C.

Death of Socrates or no death of Socrates, classicism spread, and informed the evolution of the western world for 2,500 years. It was, after all, an extremely efficient and advantageous philosophy. The various principles of classicism provided solid ground for the development of increasingly complex forms of social organization, to which we owe all our great achievements, whether political, medical, technological, etc.; over time, this helped overthrow the tyranny of the despot, and paved the way for our modern conception of democratic-republican government. But something changed in the 19th century: Marx had imagined a counter-philosophy rooted in resentment toward the ruling class, though western governments were already transitioning from monarchy to democracy all across the European-American world. Marx called this resentment "the liberation of the proletariat;" it was nothing of the sort. Because the very success of the classical tradition was itself a problem for Marx: Gone were the (imagined) days of agrarian "equality" (which was merely universal poverty); capitalism had amplified complexity and therefore stratification.

To the mind of Marx, success of *this* individual was impossible without suppression of *that* individual. He was trying to imagine a solution to the problems of the *old* social system; he did not appear to understand that capitalism was itself a solution to those very same problems. Despite the fact that capitalism results in a better quality of life even for the poor, he was incapable of imagining a non-zero sum scenario. For Marx, the only thing that mattered was how power was divided up in society. Advancements in material prosperity were irrelevant; only *the apportionment* of those advancements was important to Marx.

Marx was driven by an instinctual animosity. He was *compelled* towards the overthrow of capitalism. Ironically, it was the very system that he himself was privileged to live in. Marx was born into a family of rabbis and lawyers; he was *bourgeoisie,* and his wife Johanna von Westphalen was petty nobility, and thus *bourgeoisie* as well. Nevertheless, he took on the mantle of the proletariat…

Whether he understood his own hypocrisy can only be guessed at.

But *how* does one overthrow an entire economic system? And more importantly, *what* does one replace it with, exactly? Ideologies develop societies through behavioral feedback loops: *This* system impacts behavior differently than *that* system impacts behavior. Whatever the system, human beings respond to the incentives and disincentives of their social systems. These are either positive or negative; some systems complement human nature better than others. Marx knew this well enough (though he *overestimated* the malleability of human nature by many orders of magnitude); he knew that if his philosophy were to actually overthrow the old order, the entire worldview of the old order must first be condemned. Because the old order had to go, classicism had to go as well.

From its beginning, Marxism represented a reversal of values. It represents vengefulness towards the powerful in pseudo-philosophical form, and finds its expression through economic envy. If the Marxist were honest, he would declare openly: "That man possesses something that I do not possess. But *why* should I not possess it as well? This is due entirely to chance; it is therefore an injustice to say that he deserves it! And so somebody must take it from him and give it to me, which is only fair, after all…"

But the Marxist is *not* honest; he does not even know *himself.*

Really, it should come as no surprise that Marxists have always been fascinated by psychology. The manipulation of emotion is the metaphorical bread and butter of Marxism; without the manipulation of emotion- especially *envy*-, there is no Marxism. Because in order for Marxism to prevail, it must successfully fuse two concepts eternally at odds with one another: the *words* of liberty and the *deeds* of tyranny- and it does so as straightforwardly as Pavlov himself. The method is simplistic enough: Merely pair the two concepts until they result in the same reaction. There is no *reason* in it; reason would fail. Instead, there is only raw habituation gained through the unscrupulous manipulation of the human being as though he were a dog or a pig or a rat.

The words Marxists use almost always entail exactly *the opposite* of their original and intended meanings. For a kind of Orwellian doublethink is necessary in order for Marxism to reign. Marxism has been shown to be an abject failure worldwide, yet it must be presented before the masses as though it were the solution to all the problems of the world. Such a belief requires *blindness to reason;* it requires the hysterical fanaticism of a religious zealot- and indeed, Marxism is entirely religious in its tone and tempo. And it is that very religiosity that makes Marxism such an excellent tool for usurping authority; it is also why Marxism is so adamantly anti-religion: *It will not suffer competition.*

Marxism now bears a thousand titles: relativism, materialism, secularism, feminism, globalism, internationalism, intersectionalism, and of course, post-modernism. All these belong together. Because all of these exist only *in contradistinction to* the classical tradition. They possess no identities of their own; they are entirely dependent upon the old order insofar as they are *merely reactionary.* Indeed, if the old order were abolished, their goals would vanish; their entire worldview would self-destruct. Classicism, however, is capable of standing on its own because the classical tradition stands rooted in *reality:* For the classicist, *the real world* actually exists, and so the validity of a concept can be judged accordingly without resort to questions pertaining to the speaker's category- sex, race, creed, etc. It is not a matter of perspective.

Marxism can be extremely seductive: It flatters the primitive instincts; it makes appeal to envy as well as to ambition. Truth, right and wrong, mastery of the self, a sense of personal moral responsibility- such ideals ensure a future, but do not appeal to the ego. Classicism is in this sense quintessentially positivistic in that it affirms that such-and-such is *fact*- and demands that we behave accordingly. This demand, however, is absent in Marxism, which is quintessentially negativistic: Marxism *negates;* it affirms nothing. And because of this lack of affirmation, it also *requires* nothing- no strength, no wisdom, and no compassion.

Marxism is for the weak, broken, resentful.

The very lack of ideological imperative that makes Marxism so appealing to the masses also leaves a philosophical void at the heart of the human being, and this void will destroy a society more certainly than any weapon. Marxism not only *leads to* nihilism; it *is* nihilism, and can result in nothing but self-annihilation. It is both illogical *and* unnatural. Because of this, sustaining a Marxist social system requires constant top-down control; it requires an unending war against the human condition. Anything that may reveal the truth represents a threat to the entire system. And this is why communism and socialism *always* result in tyranny: They lack the resiliency that comes from a solid foundation in truth. Whatever is old, whatever is ancient or esteemed- *that* must be destroyed.

To summarize: What we are discussing is primarily a *psychological* orientation, and it is represented all along the political spectrum, though to varying degrees. Psychologically speaking, Neo-Nazis, social justice warriors, and members of certain fundamentalist religious groups such as the Westboro Baptist Church, are all of the same breed; they are steeped in contempt for the classical tradition, and entirely ruled by their passions. However, insofar as the left has become the proverbial dog being wagged by its post-modern tail, it has become more susceptible to its effects. In the future, a very different discussion may be necessary; let us hope not.

The pendulum continues to swing…

Most of life is a feedback loop. We act, and we see that there is a result; we learn something (we hope!), and adjust accordingly. Breaking that cycle can be difficult precisely because, like an ouroboros with its tail in its mouth, it has no beginning, no place to leap into and no place to leap out from. So what is the answer to the question of how the broken soul *un-breaks* itself? And *at scale?*

We must become *masters* of ourselves once again; we must accept the truth, and act accordingly. But above all, we must never quit, never retreat, never surrender. For we are made in the image of God, after all.

And God does not kneel.

Joshua van Asakinda
18 June, 2018 (original) / 11 September, 2025 (updated)

WILL

The First Principle of Post-modern Psychology

"That freedom of will is an illusion, and therefore external factors are more powerful than internal factors."

There can be no discussion of human psychology without first agreeing upon certain premises, the first and most fundamental of which is freedom of will. For it is *will* that separates living beings from non-living things; it is *will* that makes a living being *an agent* rather than *an object,* and *conscious* of its agency. This consciousness in turn is the foundation for all our conceptualizations of God, right and wrong, mastery of the self, liberty, tyranny, and personal responsibility of any kind; it is thus the very foundation of civilization. Because none of these concepts are meaningful if the human being lacks freedom of will.

If we were to imagine a world without freedom of will, we would imagine a world very different from the one in which we currently exist, humanly speaking. Such a world would be radically mechanistic; it would be utterly irrational to entertain moral sentiments of any kind whatsoever. Just as it is nonsensical to condemn a shark for being a shark, it would be equally nonsensical to condemn a rapist for being a rapist or a murderer for being a murderer. After all, the shark is simply acting in accord with its natural programming, and if there is no freedom of will, then the rapist and the murderer are simply acting in accord with their natural programming as well.

Therefore, all of our conceptions of truth, right and wrong, and morality in its general sense, are contingent upon freedom of will. These conception in turn provide a foundation for civilization; without them, the human species would be condemned to perpetual savagery. For civilization is nothing if not a set of codes that separate the human being from the rest of the animal kingdom, and so assist in the development of the species. Without freedom of will and its moral consequences, behavior is merely a set of inputs and their necessary logical outputs, and there is no morality in that. In such a world, man *is* machine; moreover, *he cannot be otherwise.* So without agreement upon the primacy of freedom of will, any and all logical discussion pertaining to the psychology of the human being as such becomes nonsensical; we would spend our time as well discussing why marbles do this or do that.

Without respect for freedom of will as a concept, psychology ceases to be the most *human* of all sciences and becomes instead something insidious, for the condemnation of freedom of will is the condemnation of man *as a human being,* and is therefore a condemnation of humanity itself. And indeed, we do see such madness today, for the modern university is filled to the brim with extremely influential academics who argue just this, that there is no freedom of will, and thus also no consciousness- an interesting argument, considering that they at least appear to be making it consciously. But perhaps we have given them too much credit; perhaps the zombies among us are not merely metaphorical. Regardless, there seems there is no end to the mischief an academic can get himself into when he has nothing better to do- and our professional academics rarely have something better to do.

The history of this idiocy dates back well over a century, and its rudimentary theoretical precursors date back thousands of years. Today, the question of consciousness is most often discussed in the realm of philosophy, especially philosophy as it pertains to artificial intelligence, where it is, if nothing else, an interesting thought experiment. However, there is sometimes a very wide gap between theory and the practical application of theory, and when this idea is applied to the real world, it is truly catastrophic. For no man is morally responsible for anything that he has no power to alter, and if man has no freedom of will, then he has no power to alter anything whatsoever; he is therefore no longer *morally responsible* for his own thoughts, feelings, and behaviors. But when this occurs, the human being has abdicated his own humanity; he ceases to be human, and becomes instead a cog in a machine, a wheel or a screw- and little better than that. Moreover, when the human being *as an individual* has so been reduced, the human being *as a unit of organization* has likewise been reduced; the foundation of civilization itself has been brought into question- and is soon abolished entirely.

This result has rarely been the intended aim of philosophers, and yet it just so happens to be the only natural logical consequence of a philosophy hell-bent on abandoning a non-deterministic worldview. The thirst for a purely mechanistic philosophy, one in which there is no God, no human soul, and no freedom of will, has resulted in the disruption of the causal chain leading to personal responsibility. After all, how can a man be held accountable for his thoughts, feelings, and behaviors when his thoughts, feelings, and behaviors are entirely outside his control? Therefore, is his hypothesized machine-like nature not sufficient to absolve him entirely of responsibility?

It is indeed sufficient.

In this, at least, post-modern philosophy entails a certain degree of logical consistency. For the post-modernist follows the causal chain perfectly- whether he knows it or not-, and he rarely stops to question or to complain. It is as though he fell asleep at the beginning of a journey only to awake halfway through; he does not know the path behind, but he follows the path ahead nonetheless. And oddly enough, he does not even ask where the path is leading…

Like every lemming before him, the modern-day progressive follows the path of *non*-willing because, after all, what can he do? He himself possesses *no will* (or so he thinks); he cannot determine another path. This belief- or rather, this *lack* of belief (again, Marxism and its various bastard ideologies are rooted entirely in *negation*)- is so poisonous that it strives to validate and to legitimize any and all paths leading unto self-destruction. Because once again, *if* it is true that man possesses no will, *what can he do?* Why even *try to rebel* against such machine-like necessity?

This despair, this hopelessness in the face of a falsity believed to be factual, becomes obvious when we examine the solutions proposed by the progressive to everyday problems: Without exception, there is always *an external agent* to be blamed; *the internal agent* is never even brought into the discussion. In other words, the causal chain always begins in *the world;* the individual himself bears no responsibility whatsoever. Instead, his guilt is attributed to God, or to nature, or to circumstance, or to society- but it is *never* attributed *to the individual.* This is proof enough how far the *intelligentsia* has fallen from the truth.

When this state of affairs has finally been accepted as gospel, the human being is no longer an authority over himself. He becomes a slave; he *can be* nothing *but* a slave. What else would we call a man who has had his freedom removed from him? Whether his freedom has been stolen by an external agent or abdicated voluntarily makes no difference in the end; the voluntary abdication of freedom results in a slavery no less real.

For it is the responsibility that comes with freedom of will that defines the human being; with the abdication of that responsibility comes the abdication of humanity itself. There is simply no getting around this fact. This is why in ancient Greece, the birthplace of the European classical tradition, there was so much discussion of will, and especially insofar as it relates to reason. And so Socrates in his optimism had argued that man's immorality was rooted merely in *ignorance of the good;* Aristotle later disagreed, arguing instead that man is not only driven by *reason* but also by *passion-* that these passions want fulfillment as well, and that the conflict between these two drives contributes to our various counter-productive thoughts, feelings, and behaviors. So for Aristotle, man ought to strive for *enkrateia* (ἐγκράτεια)- literally, "to be in power [over oneself]," for when man fails to achieve *enkrateia,* he slips into another and opposing condition: *akrasia* (ἀκρασία)- literally, "to be lacking in command [over oneself]." Through *akrasia,* the passions are left unbridled, and man, even when knowing the good, may thus be rendered too weak to choose it.

This is essentially what we see in the world today, only the situation has grown far more dangerous because of the near universal adoption by academics of post-modern gibberish ("intersectionality" and the like), which half-baked pseudo-intellectuals use as a bludgeoning tool in order to condemn reasoned arguments for which they have no answer. As a result, we now live in a world in which men are not only *ignorant* of truth, and *too weak* to choose the good, but a world in which *they do not even believe that the good exists at all-* and so they do not even bother developing either the wisdom or the strength of willpower necessary in order to seek it, to defend it, to nourish it. This is a problem of an entirely different order; it is a disaster of enormous proportions, epic in scale and scope. For man has now voluntarily abdicated the path to his own fulfillment, and he does not even know it. Worse, this abdication has more often than not been rooted in trickery: He has been *lied to,* and as a result of that deception, something utterly irreplaceable has been stolen from him. But he has been told that it is for the best; he has been raised from womb to tomb entrapped by that deception. He does not know that it is a Mephistophelean pact: The abolition of the will is the de-identification of the individual with his own agency as an individual in return for all the social immunity that comes with victimhood, which results in what may appear at first glance to be a short-term benefit: to never be responsible for one's own failures ("I am blameless *no matter what!*"). However, the final consequences, as with any Mephistophelean pact, are truly horrifying…

CONFLICT

The Second Principle of Post-modern Psychology

"That because external factors are more powerful than internal factors, competition and its resulting hierarchies must be inherently unjust."

The indoctrination of *akrasia* is perhaps the greatest of all evils, for it robs the human being of his humanity before he even has an opportunity to develop it. Moreover, the consequences of this evil are far-reaching, and have an affect at every level of civilization, specifically because it destroys the very foundation upon which all civilization is predicated. For what happens to the man who is no longer master *of himself?* He is soon confronted with reality, and with the realization that he is no longer master *of anything.*

We are usually taught to think of tyranny in terms of *external* oppressors. However, *internal* oppressors exist as well, and are far more insidious; they rule our thoughts, feelings, and behaviors as assuredly as any dictator- and even more so because *we do not know it.* What is really fundamental for the establishment of civilization is not so much liberation from *external* tyranny as liberation from *internal* tyranny. Man must be, first and foremost, *master of himself,* else there can be no civilization no matter what the structure of society may be. After all, what does it matter what laws are passed to govern man if man is not capable of governing himself enough to follow the law?

However, in the case of Marxism and its various downstream ideologies, the natural order has been turned on its head. He that finds himself bound by progressive pseudo-psychology is no longer master either of himself or of his passions (for his passions are a part of him); he must therefore submit- and be ground to dust. There is no romanticizing the truth: The passions are *terrifying* (the word *passion,* after all, means "to suffer"). And a terrifying thing it is to be torn apart from the inside out...

The result of post-modern philosophy, or any other philosophy not rooted firmly in the classical tradition, is the submission of man before the passions, and thus a return to so many thousands of years of pre-civilization savagery. So why would a man submit to such an ideology? What could possibly attract him to a philosophy so deeply rooted in his own self-destruction? Clearly, no man in his right mind would willfully abdicate his own humanity- but once again we find that post-modernists have pulled the wool over the eyes of anybody foolish enough to take the bait.

A fundamental tenet of Marxist thought is *conflict between classes.* Taken in and of itself, there may be something to the notion that various classes may be locked in some sort of *near*-zero sum game (this assertion is up for debate, but outside the scope of this book). However, the progressive takes a logical leap, assuming a causal relationship that cannot be demonstrated: The progressive believes that class *inequality* is "proof" of class *oppression,* and that this oppression must be eradicated (to the benefit of the proletariat, of course). But these terms are not *synonymous,* and so the assertion implies a causal chain that cannot be demonstrated. Perhaps inequality and oppression do exist together, but then, so do tigers and vipers; it does not follow that the one is the cause of the other merely because they coexist. Consequently, it also does not follow that the eradication of the one will result in the eradication of the other.

"By eradicating inequality, we will eradicate oppression!" That is a sleight of hand, and not at all demonstrable. Individuals are *not* equal; left to their own devices, their outcomes will *not* be equal either. And so there is no necessary relationship between the two concepts whatsoever. This explains Marxism's many failures: It never addresses the root of the very problem that it claims to be interested in solving, even if we assume "the good intentions" of the Marxist.

Moreover, post-modern philosophy implies- perhaps unknowingly- that a static social system is *desirable.* Because any movement at all, any growth or any stress, any development of any kind on the part of any individual whatsoever, would immediately result in an inequality of some kind- and that inequality is proof of oppression, according to Marx. Therefore, in order for equality to be maintained, all these would have to be *forbidden*- all movement, all growth and all stress, all development of the individual. And so it becomes clear that post-modernism, taken as an imperative, precludes adaptation; it is the enemy of evolution both at the personal level and at the systemic level.

Living systems are *dynamic*. There is no permanent stability in a dynamic system; all dynamic systems are inherently *unequal* in their distribution of resources. Physicists will testify, any energetic system that achieves universal equilibrium ceases to be *life-sustaining;* it may even cease to exist *at all*. Therefore, the conditions for life at the most fundamental scales *require inequality*- and not *only* at the most fundamental scales. The same principle applies to *every* scale of reality, from the cosmological to the biological, and from the biological to the psychological. And so any worldview predicated upon the notion that the equalization of resources is a logical possibility (as Marxism is)- or that this mythic equalization ought to constitute a kind of moral imperative to re-structure the world anew (as the Marxist believes)- is doomed to failure from the very beginning because it ignores the fundamental nature of reality itself. Nowhere in nature do we find equality; neither do we find it in culture: Resources (power, money, women, etc.) have never been equally distributed, nor will they ever be equally distributed- and yet, *the idea* of equality remains…

One might reasonably ask how an idea can persist when all available evidence stands in contradiction to it. Simply stated, the idea flatters the ego; it justifies whatever passion one prefers while asking nothing of value in return. Furthermore, seeing through the deception requires self-examination, and the ego has no interest in self-examination. It is eternally unconcerned with truth; it is only concerned with the survival of the self in the genetic sense of survival. And so whatever brings this aim into question- the truth included- is, from the point of view of the ego, the enemy, and must be destroyed.

This ego-centric orientation is typical of progressive psychology insofar as the progressive rarely thinks in terms of *truth*-quality; instead, the progressive thinks in terms of *threat*-quality. For the Marxist, it is not whether or not a fact, theory, worldview, ideology is *verified* that matters but rather whether or not it is *dangerous*. Post-modernism, after all, is essentially the subordination of intellect to emotion. And this makes sense considering the fact that post-modernism as a movement denies that there is any freedom of will, and so whoever espouses it learns quickly to doubt his own ability to defend himself against enemies.

Whatever threatens the ego- *whether it is true or not*- must be destroyed. But who will do the destroying when the progressive does not believe *in his own will?* There is only one logical conclusion: *The world itself* must protect him. Or so he thinks…

Clearly, "the world" will not protect him, for "the world" is merely shorthand for other individuals who also have their own egos to protect, and so *this* individual is rarely concerned with *that* individual; each has his own agenda. But we must remember that post-modernism externalizes the locus of responsibility so that it must *always* be an external agent that accomplishes anything, right or wrong. This reorientation of responsibility illuminates the discrepancy between what Marxists *claim to support,* which is *liberty,* and what their belief system *actually results in,* which is *tyranny.* The progressive (at least at the bottom of the hierarchy) probably *does* desire "liberty" in some fashion, but he has been indoctrinated not believe that he- or anyone else, for that matter- possesses the freedom of will necessary in order to ensure it. And so for the progressive, freedom can never be a *personal* question; it must always be a *political* question. Tragically, the result is that the progressive lives in some sense under a two-fold tyranny: He is crushed not only by the tyranny of his own lack of ability to direct his own life but also by the tyranny of a world that he has been indoctrinated to believe ought to protect him but does not.

This latent self-realization of powerlessness entirely explains the hysterical need for progressives *to feel protected* (i.e., to be given a "safe space" because "words are violence," and so forth). When the individual has been tricked into abandoning his freedom of will, everything in the world becomes a threat in need of neutralization, which necessitates an ever-growing scope of necessary protections. And yet these protections never really address the problem, which is the disintegration of the will of the individual, and so his hysteria increases exponentially over time, which in turn results in even more strident calls for protection; these also fail, and the cycle continues. Paradoxically, this cycle results in a far more oppressive social system than ever would have existed if men had just been allowed to freely compete amongst themselves.

Clearly, in any system where resources are allocated unequally, there will be, for lack of better terms, "victors" and "victims," those who have a relatively greater quantity of resources and those who have a relatively smaller quantity of resources. This state of affairs, however, can result in a generally better society for all involved- an assertion the progressive denies. Because the progressive views *all* inequality in *non-zero-sum terms,* and since he perceives this apparent non-zero-sum situation as a threat, his only possible response is the call for more and more radical manipulation of the system: more government, more legislation, and more tyrannization. For this reason among others, Marxism *always* results in tyranny, and cannot result in anything *but* tyranny.

Ultimately, because the progressive does not believe in his own freedom of will, he fears conflict, and thus requires systematic protections. Were the veil of madness miraculously pulled from his eyes, he would perhaps see that he possesses freedom of will, that conflict is a necessity of reality, and that there is no injustice in inequality- for inequality is merely a function of reality. Everyone alive begins with a different set of circumstances; this is simply how the game works, and yet the progressive has been indoctrinated to believe that he should be able to win the game without understanding the rules. And so he continues to fail; cognitive dissonance sets in, and he comes to the conclusion that the game is rigged. Despite his refusal to learn the rules and to play the game better, he blames the world for his failure. Consequently, he becomes more radical over time in his desire to re-design the rules of the game, which results inevitably in the kind of violent revolution that Marxist movements are so well known for.

The progressive feels the weight of immense oppression- actual *and* artificial-, but that sensitivity is rooted in his own *internal* condition and is only then projected *externally* upon the world. For the world appears to be more and more frightening the more the individual abdicates his own will. This results in the progressive demanding large-scale changes to society that never come, and if they *did* by some miracle come, they would never fix the problem because he has completely misdiagnosed the source of his own misery. And so the vicious cycle continues: less will, more fear, failed solution; less will, more fear, failed solution; less will, more fear, failed solution; and on and on and on, *ad infinitum...*

It should come as no surprise to anyone that this ultimately results in the kind of screaming-at-the-sky madness we sometimes see in our youth today. The progressive makes demands upon the world while simultaneously denying in theory that any individual within the world possesses the agency necessary in order to fulfill those very same demands. Such a situation does not intersect in any way with reason, and moreover, it *anthropomorphizes* reality: It constitutes a kind of moral-magical thinking, for although it is completely and totally rational to maintain expectations for the actions of *individuals,* it makes less than zero sense to maintain expectations for how *billions of individuals* ought to act *as a singular organization.* That is an utterly fantastical view of reality.

"The world *ought to be* such-and-such; the world *ought not to be* such-and-such"- so thinks the speck of dust before he is blown away by the wind, never to be remembered. The world has *no concern whatsoever* for "oughts" and "ought nots;" in fact, it has no concerns of any kind. Whatever our moral judgments, they exist on a very different level than reality itself, and so there is often very little in the way of intersection between them. For most of human history, a Venn diagram illustrating the relationship between *what is* and *what ought to be* would entail *no overlap whatsoever.* And so retroactively applying moral judgments to the workings of reality itself is not an effective strategy for living in the world.

In order to function well in the world, the individual must begin with an appreciation for truth, not only in the sense of *not lying* but also and especially in the sense of *perceiving things as they really are.* This is an exceptionally difficult talent to acquire, especially since, as we have already discussed, the ego is concerned primarily with preserving the ego- *and the ego lies.* Moreover, it can be tricky to learn to overcome the ego because we only learn *via* the ego. Such a paradox carries with it many questions, for it would seem we are all caught in a trap, and yet we must all at some point or other *leap out...*

This is the essential difference between the classical worldview and the modernist worldview: The classicist sees that reality *is* such-and-such *and strategizes accordingly* while the modernist refuses to see reality as such-and-such and so perpetuates his own victimhood, forever at the mercy of his own unwillingness to recognize his true potential as a human being, as a being *capable of overcoming adversity.* Tragically, if he were to set aside his self-pity for even a moment, he would perhaps realize that when the world is taken for what it is, it becomes much easier to formulate practical solutions to problems. But so long as he remains fixated on fantasies- which are really all his various "oughts" and "ought nots" amount to-, there is no room left for solutions. After all, no man can hope to win a game in which he refuses to learn the rules.

Fortune is not fair. Each of us begins his journey with a different set of circumstances, and each of us must contend with his own enemies, and each of us must pass through his own trials and tribulations. Life is *conflict:* Each serves his own interests, which rarely align, and so some become victors and some become victims. This may sound like a brutal way of looking at things, but it is far more rational- not to mention far more strategic- to address the situation *as it is* than to demand of the world *that it be otherwise.* For it is by demanding that the world be otherwise- and by seeing that it never is- that we modern citizens of the western world have become so *unfulfilled,* and in spite of enjoying more prosperity than nine-tenths of the population of the planet!

In some sense, the degree to which a person is capable of recognizing truth- especially *hard truth* pertaining to adversity-, and of strategizing accordingly in order to overcome that adversity, is the degree to which he is capable of developing *a victor psychology* rather than *a victim psychology.* Truth, therefore, and the manner in which the individual approaches truth, the quality of his relationship with truth- and not any particular set of circumstances, as we have been told- is the primary determinant factor of intellectual and emotional stability. Because the ability to face the world *as it is* rather than *as one might wish it to be* is at the very heart of psychological wellbeing, and its absence may as well be the definition of psychological dysfunction. If any society is ever to maintain control of its own destiny, it must never cease to uphold a worldview that recognizes this.

Progressives, of course, argue otherwise, and have done so persuasively (though fallaciously). Why, though? How could an idea so obviously at odds with the flourishing of the human being continue to grow, like a cancer? Because the truth remains, inexorable: *Men that cannot direct themselves are easily led about.* And Marxism has proven itself precocious in this regard: It excels in creating slaves, men of little value that are easily led about.

But it should not be forgotten that most progressives are not at fault for their modernism; they have been indoctrinated since childhood to hold the most precious quality of their own humanity in contempt. They have been deceived, manipulated. So in truth, they really *are* victims in a certain sense- but they misattribute *the source* of their victimhood: They believe that it comes *from the world* instead of *from within themselves.* For it is *their own philosophy* that oppresses them- and those that poisoned them with it.

The result of two or three generations of Marxist-inspired pedagogy has been mass-cultural freefall into perpetual fear, a habitual tendency towards threat-perception, and all the irrational consequences that follow from such a disorderly state of internal affairs. Now the proposals for solving these problems continually and necessarily increase in scale and scope, thus resulting in ever-increasingly intrusive social control. But all these so-called "solutions" fail- indeed, they *must* fail- because they completely miss the point: The solution to the problem lies *within* and *not without.*

This sad lack of accurate problem-analysis explains exactly why so many Marxists condemn conflict: They have no answer for Marxism's many inconsistencies, nor for its many undesirable outcomes, and so they claim that if only the conditions for Marxism could be made perfect, then it would function as imagined. Of course, a theory that can only function under perfect circumstances is not a very good theory. Nevertheless, Marxists bow before a Liberal Trinity that they believe are sufficient to re-engineer the world, a tiny trio of new gods- Feminism, Pacifism, and Nihilism. Their goal is simply the total annihilation of the classical worldview (that damned monkey wrench!), or to put it in simpler terms: "No men, no war, and no God to fight it for." And once such a world has been arranged, there will be nobody to rebel, no rebellion, and no reason *for* rebellion, which will, they believe, fix the problem.

(It will not, of course, but they *believe* that it will).

All this philosophizing, however, continues to amount to nothing; all these clever machinations and social engineering schemes continue to come up empty-handed. After all, no amount of magical thinking can transform the world into something that it is not. Consequently, the discrepancy between the world *as it is* and the world *as the progressive wishes it to be* persists, the cognitive dissonance continues to mount, the psychological tension continues to grow more pronounced, the feeling that "Something is wrong!" grows progressively stronger and more violent. But the question as to *why* all these well-intended fantasies continually fail is never really answered, leading the progressive to the inevitable conclusion that *the world itself* is unjust, that *the system itself* is rigged against him, and that he is therefore the victim of a grand conspiracy- and this is the cause of much resentment.

VENGEFULNESS

The Third Principle of Post-modern Psychology

"That because inequality is inherently unjust, the possession of power is itself an act of oppression, and justifies a violent reaction."

The psychology of the victor assumes some degree of separation between *the external world* and *the internal world* in that the victor is capable of maintaining a sense of sovereignty over his internal conditions *regardless* of external circumstances; the psychology of the victim, however, is characterized instead by difficulty in separating the external world from the internal world because the victim lacks any *sense of sovereignty over himself* whatsoever. For when self-mastery has been removed from the scenario- and in the mind of the victim, *it has*- the boundary between external and internal becomes blurred: *The self loses its sense of self.* And so the victim comes to consider himself perpetually at the mercy of the world- and to some degree, *he is right.*

Locus of responsibility- whether the causes of one's thoughts, feelings, and behaviors are held to be primarily *internal* (the *classical* worldview) or to be primarily *external* (the *modernist* worldview)- might perhaps be the best proxy for measuring mental health in the world today. The man who possesses agency over his internal world knows *what is self* and *what is not self;* the man who does not, however, has difficulty detaching himself from external influences. For the man capable of effective agency, no matter how difficult his circumstances, he is able to maintain some sense of *unviolated self-identity;* he can adjust to circumstances as necessary. But the case is very different when self-mastery has been abandoned: The man who lacks effective agency cannot let go of the world because *his identity* is entirely wrapped up in external objects; he perceives- quite wrongly, but nonetheless- that the root of his thoughts, feelings, and behaviors is *not his own.* Because of this, he cannot be content, for he can never gain possession of himself. Surely, there are moments of pleasure: When the world gives him "happiness," he experiences "happiness" (or what he has been *conditioned to experience* as happiness), and when the world gives him "suffering," he experiences "suffering" (or what he has been *conditioned to experience* as suffering). But whether he experiences the one or the other is of little relevance; in either case, he is not in control- and at some level, *he knows it.*

It is the sense of control over oneself and over one's internal condition that allows one to transcend the pendulum of happiness and suffering, and instead to attain a sense of fulfillment in the face of either. But an abiding equanimity cannot be achieved by means of externals; it is absolutely *an internal phenomenon.* Such a condition can only be achieved through a long-habituated sense of personal responsibility, with all the struggles and hard-fought successes that personal responsibility inevitably entails. And that is the Holy Grail of psychology.

However, the man who has been nourished on a daily diet of post-modernism cannot find this fulfillment anywhere specifically because he is always oriented *towards the external world.* Thus, contentment continually evades him. "Something must be wrong," he thinks, whether he is a millionaire celebrity in Hollywood or an ultra-affluent student at the University of Berkeley, still he senses oppression *everywhere*- and even believes *that he himself is oppressed!* Yet he has done everything *right* (that is, *left*): He has read the right anti-American books; he has made the right soy-drinking friends in all the right gun-hating cities; he has studied at the right universities and he has been granted the right degree in Caucasian-hating gender studies; he has gotten the right job doing nothing for too much money, with the right lofty goal of "changing things;" he has bought the right 20-mile per hour electric box on donut wheels; he has choked down the right over-priced organic food from whateverpopulargibberish.com; he has watched the right socially conscientious movies full of actors from marginalized demographics; he has felt pity for the right darkly-skinned people, and of course for those blessed with a goddess-vagina; he has stood with the right feminists while never having sex with any of them in order to prove that he is different from "all the other men™;" he has worn the right rainbow-colored onesie to the right gay pride parades; he has voted for the right left-wing politicians that have all regurgitated the right politically-correct talking points; he has called for the right tax increases that would only apply to *the right somebody else;* he has condemned the right capitalists on social media through his thousand dollar iPhone; he has hated the right "hateful bigots;" he has threatened to murder the right Second Amendment supporters; he has bravely fought the right peaceful war against the right straight/white/male oppressors on Twitter; he has raged in silent contempt at the right person staring back at him in the mirror; he has done everything right, just as he was told to do- *and so why is he still angry and malcontent?*

"Something must be wrong…"

Such an astonishing lack of self-awareness only proves that no amount of opportunity can erase the sense of enslavement at the bottom of progressive psychology. Paradoxically, this very sense of enslavement results in exactly its opposite- that typical, pervasive *sense of entitlement* common to children and old spoiled brats, which is itself nothing more than a reflex reaction, the ego's desire to reassert itself at the tail end of a losing battle, to perhaps recover some small iota of *self-esteem* and *self-empowerment.* Tragically, the slavery that the progressive claims to experience is in fact real, but he misidentifies the slave-master. For the slave-master is not *in the world* at all. The slave-master is *within;* the slave-master is *the ego itself,* or rather, the *anarchy* that exists where the ego rules (or *claims* to rule). The ego, after all, enjoys satisfying the passions specifically because the passions are *rooted in the ego,* and the ego, therefore, does not want to restrain its various lusts and needs and wants; it desires rather to satisfy them all. But this desire entails a sophisticated self-deception, for it is not possible for any of these lusts and needs and wants *to ever be* satisfied. They are, as all the saints have known, "like ravening fires," and *they will destroy whatever they touch, including him whose lusts and needs and wants they belong to.*

In the end, the man who is not in control of himself finds himself consumed by his own consumption. The ego seeks only *to serve itself* and *to preserve itself,* and thereby paradoxically sows the seeds of its own destruction. It is utterly myopic; it possesses no foresight whatsoever. Because the ego- like everything else in this world- has been destined to pass away; all the passions of the ego are likewise destined to pass away, and so too the objects of those passions (power, money, women, etc.). But the progressive does not recognize this, and in fact *cannot* recognize this, because his entire worldview *denies* the fact that truth can be known *at all.*

When a man has gained control over himself, nothing can press him into slavery. He may be *murdered,* yes, but he cannot be *enslaved;* whatever his fate, he remains ultimately free. Contrarily, when a man has no control over himself, he lives forever in slavery no matter his situation. For the operating factor of freedom is an *internal* locus of responsibility, and *not* particular conditions or circumstances as is generally proposed. Now, that is not to say that the cultivation of self-mastery *ensures* material success of any kind, but it *does* ensure the *promise of peace* in the midst of trial and tribulation, which we all must overcome in any event, each in his own way. After all, "happiness" and "suffering" are *relative,* and there is no measure by which the happiness or suffering of one can be compared to the happiness or suffering of another. Ultimately, such concepts are entirely subjective; they possess *no objective truth-value whatsoever.*

Still, the human condition- and therefore the human experience- presumes *some* degree of materiality, and to some extent, the world is a realm of passions and of the satisfaction of passions. As members of the animal kingdom, we share in the instincts and impulses of all other animals: We want to live, hunt, feed, breed, and reign. These drives have sustained our species in the face of perpetual near-extinction for many thousands of years, as they have every other species on the planet. But the human being is a very *special* kind of animal, and in addition to these basic desires, he also possesses something superior to all these, which is of course the capacity for self-mastery.

It is *self-mastery* that makes us *human;* it is self-mastery that makes us *more than animal-* if only we can cultivate it within ourselves. Success in this regard is not at all a given. Self-mastery is rare, yet it is an achievement worth striving for, if only for the fact that it is only through striving for it that we can discover ourselves. And so it is *self-mastery* that separates the *classical* worldview from the *modernist* worldview; it is *self-mastery* that offers the surest path to the flourishing and fulfillment of the individual. The progressive, of course, believes otherwise…

For the Marxist, the solution to all of our problems exists *out there,* somewhere, *in the world.* The problem, he argues, is "systemic" (his most favorite word of all!); its solution must therefore be "systemic" as well. He has no faith in himself, nor faith in his own strength of will; he only has faith in that quasi-mystical *system* known as "society." But man cannot realize his meaning in the world without first knowing *himself,* as it is precisely this penetration into *his own inner being* that provides him insight into the revelation that *he is something more than merely an animal.* All our virtue- all our strength, wisdom, and compassion- derives from this. Post-modern psychology, however, makes it impossible to know the self because it directs the attention of the individual *away* from the *internal* world and *towards* the *external* world- and then *fixes it there* as the sole source of all meaning.

This becomes clear when we examine the most popular forms of therapy in the world today: drugs, false self-esteem, and no personal responsibility whatsoever. Our current paradigm of modern psychology destroys individuals through the destruction of their agency *as* individuals. And this *destruction of self-agency,* which is itself *quintessentially Marxist,* might be sufficient to explain the resentment that rests at the bottom of modern- that is, *post-modern-* "liberalism:" It has grown deep and toxic, a raging vindictiveness directed against whatever is strong, healthy, virtuous (i.e., whatever is *classical*). That raging vindictiveness is not without cause, however: The modern progressive is vengeful because he is *empty,* and worse, *at least unconsciously aware of his emptiness.*

A great injustice has in fact been perpetrated: The will of the human being has been *abolished.* But this sense of injustice has been entirely manipulated in order to aim it as a weapon not only against those that have convinced entire generations of human beings to abdicate their own self-agency in the name of progress but also against those that have refused to do so! Such a grand level of manipulation cannot be accidental; it is entirely *intentional,* not to mention *insidious.* For *he who believes that he has no will does not rebel.*

Progressives, steeped as they are in post-modern contradiction and thus despite all claims to the contrary, are absolutely *obsessed* with slavery, *whether they know it or not.* And indeed, they may *not* know it; so much of their own psychology lies hidden from them! The well is deep, and few of us really know who we are, yet what is most lacking in us today is also what is most necessary: *self-knowledge.* This is the beginning of wisdom, after all, inscribed as it was across the forecourt of the Temple of Apollo at Delphi: *Gnothi seauton* (Γνῶθι σεαυτόν), "Know thyself."

But the progressive does *not* know himself, *cannot* know himself.

There are few at the bottom of the modern liberal hierarchy who ever question whether those at the top have *genuinely* good intentions; instead, the overseers command and the underlings, like lemmings, all jump gleefully into the sea. This is because there are two classes of Marxists: those that lie and *know* that they are lying, and those that lie and *do not know* that they are lying. The overseer class of progressive (perhaps a tiny minority) uses "liberalism" as a tool for manipulating others; the underling class of progressive (by far the majority) is merely *useful* to the first, *but only insofar as its constituents are willing to allow themselves to be exploited by those that are higher up the chain of command.* Those at the top of the hierarchy are well aware of their deception; those at the bottom have no idea. They have merely been raised to believe, and to believe with the zealotry and fanaticism of any cultist.

But when things goes to Hell, *they eat each other.*

What may be saddest and most tragic of all is that most of our progressives would have led fulfilling lives if only they had not been ensnared by such a toxic philosophy, if only they had not been convinced that in the abdication of personal responsibility they would have found *liberation-* exactly the opposite of what is really to be found lurking there where self-agency has been abandoned. *For personal responsibility can only be abolished where freedom of will has been abolished, and where freedom of will has been abolished, humanity itself has been abolished.* This is why, when viewed from the outside looking in, progressives have always prescribed as solution *exactly the same conditions that have created the problem to be solved:* This is not merely apparent; this is the very core of post-modernism. It is an inherently *emotional-* that is, *illogical-* philosophy, and that is why its effects are universally disastrous.

Those at the top of the totem pole are well aware that the logical consequences of their worldview are undesirable to anyone but themselves, and so they claim that the path does *not* result in the goal- a claim accompanied by propaganda that flatters the egos of those below them because it is always bound up with the promise of some benefit. It is this flattery that makes post-modernism so appealing: "But it isn't *your* fault; it's *society's* fault! You, after all, *can do no wrong...*" And who among us is truthful enough to refute what he secretly wishes to be told? After all, there is no man in this world that does not secretly wonder whether the entirety of the universe revolves around *him;* we are *monsters of vanity.* Our vanity, however, is rooted in *self-deception,* and it drives us all eventually to *self-destruction.* This is inevitable; it cannot result in anything but death- and it does.

In 1880, a French socialist named Louis Auguste Blanqui published a journal called *Ni Dieu ni Maître.* This title, *"Neither God nor Master,"* perfectly sums up the post-modern attitude towards life, which is of course rooted historically in Marxism. It is a radical projection of the lack of self-mastery that lies at the root of all modernism and post-modernism, and it reveals just how pathologically obsessed the progressive (at that time, *liberal*) is with throwing off chains, which he may never truly throw off until he recognizes that his chains are *internal* rather than *external.* In purely psychological terms, the liberal's obsession with what he calls "freedom" is almost proof of his *lack* of *self-dominion.* After all, when we truly possess a thing, we rarely notice that we have it, and never clamor after its acquisition, for it has already been acquired.

We only obsess about that which we *lack*- and the progressive obsesses about one thing and one thing only: "freedom." Now, the overseer knows that his ideas are self-contradictory nonsense- or perhaps he only senses it. Perhaps it is not even *intentional;* perhaps it is merely *instinctual.* We are, after all, better at lying to *others* when we have first lied to *ourselves*- but that is no excuse. The overseer's *voluntary* actions and attitudes towards the slavery of his fellow man mean little in light of his *unconscious* actions and attitudes, all of which result in the suffocation of the very *root of freedom.* He is a *tyrant,* whether he reflects deeply upon it or not- worse, he is a *traitor,* for it is *his own followers* that he has enslaved.

There is only one inoculation sufficient to combat this cancer, and that is *truth.* For in the midst of truth, ego is given a choice: *submit* or *revolt.* Where the ego submits to truth, there is *hope;* where the ego revolts against truth, there is *none.* Ironically, he whose submits becomes *more* effective in his dealings with the world, if only because he can look at his situation more *honestly,* and thus more *strategically;* he plays the game better because he has become a more *tactical* thinker. However, where the ego revolts, it essentially doubles down on counter-productive behavior, and thus becomes virtually powerless before the world because it has thus rendered itself *incapable of responding effectively.* Whoever finds himself in such a situation has been blinded to reality, and simply *cannot* win the game; *he is doomed.* There is simply no amount of success that can ever calm the turmoil associated with remaining forever at the mercy of passions that can never be satisfied.

The modern man must admit to himself that the world, in its material sense, *is utterly indifferent to him;* he is *not* a beautiful snowflake, and the world does *not* revolve around him or his desires. When he admits this to himself, he quickly realizes that there is only one thing in this world that he can truly control, and *that is himself.* He must learn and re-learn what every great spiritual teacher has taught: *The true path is an internal experience.* The perennial philosophy of self-mastery is at the heart of all classical traditions- European *and* Oriental-, and it is the very antithesis of Marxism, modernism, post-modernism, and all their associated ideologies.

Though the progressive may often speak of "empowerment," he will rarely discuss the *causes and conditions* of that empowerment, for in acknowledging these, he would be compelled to address his own behavioral contradictions. His deepest conviction prevents self-mastery of any kind, as it condemns the validity or necessity of an unequal and imperfect world wherein self-mastery can truly be cultivated. Self-mastery requires struggle, after all; in order for it to be attained, there must first be competition, and competition implies at least a certain degree of *stratification,* a system of victors and victims- and that is hardly utopian. Therefore, since the progressive is opposed to any system of stratification *that assumes competition* (though, it should be noted, he is *not* opposed to systems of stratification slanted *artificially in his favor*), he can never *truly* become empowered.

There is a kind of selfish logic in this, as stratification necessarily implies hierarchy and the possibility for conflict and conquest, which the progressive fears due to his own incapacity when it comes to the will; he fears becoming the victim of a system that results in victors in victims- *so away with the system!* However, stratification only implies victimhood *necessarily* if the ego requires *physical victory* in order to maintain itself- and that signifies *weakness.* Typically, in cultures wherein manhood is admired, the spirit of competition is honored *even in defeat.* This the progressive does not- *cannot-* understand.

Hierarchy is quintessentially *masculine;* democracy is far more *feminine.* But because masculinity is *tribal* in character, it honors those willing *to give themselves* to the tribe, *to sacrifice themselves* for the sake of the tribe. So the principle purpose of competition is not, as the progressive imagines, the physical oppression of other human beings but rather the cultivation of mutual altruism within the ranks of a brotherhood forged in fire and consecrated by blood. For this reason, masculinity should rightly be viewed not as *egoistic* in character but rather as the most radical possible form of *anti-egoism.* Manhood does entail a willingness to kill others, if necessary- a fact that the progressive is fond of pointing out; however, manhood *also* entails a *willingness to voluntarily sacrifice oneself* for the sake of faith, family, and friendship- a fact that the progressive is *absolutely incapable* of pointing out.

Because the progressive lacks agency of his own- or at least *believes* that he does-, he naturally begins to gravitate towards groupthink. After all, he has no faith in the *individual;* he is only able to have faith in *organization,* which he hopes might, by some miracle, express that coveted freedom of will that each of its constituent parts fails to express. Strangely, although he does not believe in personal freedom of will, he does seem to believe in quasi-mystical *social* forces. This too is perfectly in line with post-modern thought, which is itself rooted so securely in the magical thinking of Marx, and his oddly illogical interpretation of history.

So the progressive, bereft of will as he is, *cannot* stand alone; he *requires* company- not out of *love* but rather in order *to feel safe.* The "loving, caring" progressive gravitates towards the group in order to feel secure just as the gazelle gravitates towards other gazelles in the hope that one of his fellow gazelles will be eaten by the lion- *but not him.* He hopes that some other individual will be sacrificed *first;* subsequently, his relationships are almost entirely *utilitarian*. Post-modernism results *necessarily* in that typical liberal tendency towards viewing other human beings merely as instruments towards some grand goal. Although this instrumentalism is deeply dehumanizing, to the mind of the progressive- which is habitually prone to reversing cause and consequence-, "grand social purpose" provides sufficient justification for any violent reaction. And as a result, it becomes obvious not only that post-modernism *may* lead to revolution, but that it post-modernism *must* lead to revolution, and in fact, *cannot* lead to anything *but* revolution.

This causal chain, though frustrating and admittedly somewhat sociopathic, is the only logical result of a worldview that denies the freedom of will- or at best merely ignores it as though it were irrelevant, as though it were but some quaint old fashioned relic of days gone by. Good intentions may in fact be a tangential motivating factor for many liberals and some progressives, but they cannot suspend the natural course of events that result from the adoption of a post-modern philosophy, which is the destruction of the human being, and of human civilization. Psychological mechanics *matter;* the nature of the human being *matters*. And any philosophy that stands in contradistinction to the nature of the human being is doomed from the very beginning. Post-modernism is one such philosophy.

The chain is clear: A lack of will results in the fear of conflict; the fear of conflict results in a psychology of vengefulness; a psychology of vengefulness results in the disintegration of society. Because the aforementioned instrumentalism that results from modern groupthink expresses itself in political theory *first* as *cult of personality,* and *finally* in the establishment- often via democratic means- of *social and political dictatorship* strong enough "to set the world on the proper path." And yet *there is no "proper path."* For where the human being has been rendered incapable of his own self-mastery, there can be *no freedom;* there is only the sacrifice of the *individual* in the name of *organization.* Then the truth is laid bare for the world to see- but it is too late: Marxism is, to steal a descriptor from Nietzsche, philosophy for *herd animals.*

And herd animals get *slaughtered.*

SOCIETY

The Fourth Principle of Post-modern Psychology

"That because individual action has not proven effective in reorganizing society, this can only be accomplished through central organization."

Humans are *social* animals, and human society is therefore largely concerned with the question of how individuals might best interact with one another. This question, however, is purely academic if human beings *as* individuals fail to cultivate their full potential *as* individuals. Because the pursuit of *a better society* is directly dependent upon the pursuit of *a better type of human being*. It is the *byproduct* of the pursuit of self-mastery, a self-mastery sufficient for the suppression of the baser and far more dominant drives, which, though useful in the short term insofar as survival is concerned, are oftentimes counterproductive to the long term goal of establishing a society in which the human being can flourish through the development of his nobler capacities.

For this reason, the establishment of *any social system* must be informed by respect for *the inner workings of the individuals,* and the individual must in turn be willing to serve other individuals through the medium of society. The relationship between the citizen and society is therefore something of a feedback loop: Nature informs culture; culture upholds nature. This is, of course, a tricky balance to maintain, and so it should be of no surprise that history is littered with failed societies. And so even at the level of civilization, it would seem that success is distributed "unfairly…"

The popular notion that societies are equal is (like most popular notions) mythology at best, and represents just one more way in which the abandonment of universal absolutes results in the most ridiculous consequences imaginable. Just as every human being is unique and no two human beings are equal in any regard, so too every society is unique and no two societies are equal in any regard. Asserting that societies are equal is to assert that the Renaissance, which has given to the world the Sistine Chapel, for instance, stands on no higher ground than Aboriginal culture, which never developed further than Stone Age technology. Such an assertion is idiotic on the face of it, surely, and yet it would be entirely consistent with the fundamental premise of post-modernism, that *"There is no truth!"* For *if* there is no truth, then surely there can be no measure of value by which to compare peoples, cultures, etc. Literally *everything* pertaining to human society is dependent upon the answer to the questions of 1. *whether truth exists,* and 2. *whether it can be known.* These answers determine whether or not the foundation of the world as we understand it has been built upon rock or upon sand.

Stated differently, *how is humanity to structure society?*

First, we must ask ourselves what the primary purpose of culture and civilization even *are:* Their primary purpose is not mere *survival* (we could survive well enough in small tribes, and *did,* for many thousands of years); rather, *it is the cultivation of humanity.* It is to increase the *trophic level* of the human being *vis-à-vis* other human beings; it is in order that the human being should flourish through society as a mediating factor, which he *cannot* do on his own. There are many points to discuss here, and so it may be instructive to address a few of them in turn: First, we can assert that society as such has some purpose; that this purpose is to cultivate their human being, to harvest something new and true from the soil of his untapped humanity; that this implies at least two phases of human development, one *preceding* cultivation in which the humanity within the human being exists only *in potential,* and one *following* cultivation in which the humanity within the human being has found expression and so *begun to flourish and to be fulfilled;* that this flourishing and fulfillment of the human being requires the cultivation of uniquely human qualities; that this flourishing and fulfillment may be retarded or distorted by social factors in contrary to those uniquely human qualities, specifically the quality of *self-mastery;* and, finally, that the harmonization of society to the human capacity for self-mastery is clearly critical to the flourishing and fulfillment of the individual.

Incidentally, the word *cultivate* comes from the Latin *cultivare,* which means "to till." Just as the nature of a specific plant determines the conditions necessary for its growth, the nature of the human being determines what kind of cultivation is correct for normal, healthy human development. Because their natures are different, what is good for the wolf is not good for the lamb and vice versa, so in order to determine what is objectively advantageous to the development of the human being, we must first study the *nature* of the human being. For any society constructed in such a way that ignores our shared humanity will thwart human development, resulting in sickness and weakness.

Thus, the question must be asked, "What defines humanity?"

If we were to survey the vastness of human society from savagery through civilization, we would see a distinct pattern form. We would discover, for instance, that *all human societies* exhibit *sex and gender roles,* and that those roles are consistent: *Males* take up positions of leadership and focus primarily on hunting and warfare; *females* take up positions of motherhood and focus primarily upon the raising of young children and the management of the home. Contrary to liberal assertions, we would also find that heterosexuality is the norm among human beings, and that *marriage* as an institution has from one end of human history to the other been defined as a relationship between males and females, even if the number of individuals within that marriage might vary (though not so much as some might imagine). We would also find that human beings require *spirituality* in order to infuse their lives with meaning, and that although the superficial qualities and characteristics of religions may vary, they all exhibit a surprising amount of agreement *insofar as their archetypes are concerned,* including the need for *moral codes* and for *mastery of the self. Reverence for ancestors,* sometimes in the form of patriarchy or patriotism, would likewise reveal itself to be a universal norm; *tribalism* too would be found everywhere just beneath the surface of social interaction, and perhaps as a corollary, the tension that arises from *in-group/out-group dynamics.* Furthermore, we would find agreement in *beauty norms:* We would find that structural symmetry is esteemed in all human cultures; we would find that biological and psychological signs indicative of traits conducive to *fatherhood* are admired everywhere in men, and that biological and psychological signs indicative of traits conducive to *motherhood* are admired everywhere in women. Similarly, we would find that *health* is always respected, and that all societies segregate those that are healthy from those that are not, *and necessarily so.*

Even in the arts we would find universal themes, for we would discover that an *appreciation for harmony* is common to all human beings, whether in the form of music, speech, or poetry. And all across the world, we would find *reverence for truth.*

All the aforementioned universals are typical of the classical tradition, which is rooted fundamentally in truth itself, in a worldview that considers the human being- usually but not always by virtue of his being created *imago Dei* (i.e., *in the image of God*)- to be morally and fundamentally *good,* and thus obligated to live up to that higher standard. For as we have mentioned, the defining quality of the human being is his capacity for *self-mastery,* his ability *to conquer himself and his own weaknesses.* This quality separates the human being from every other animal in the world; it is this quality that must be cultivated above all others, and the degree to which society promotes the cultivation of this quality is the measure of its success. And this measure makes it possible to determine which societies are *correct,* and which societies are *corrupt.*

This, of course, does not bode well for the much-dreamed-of "liberal utopia." For modern "liberalism" is predicated upon the assumption that mastery of the self is *impossible,* it has resulted in *psychological slavery-* to oneself; history; society; pressure of any kind; bad luck and unfortunate circumstances; trauma; hardship; incompetent parenting; bullying and similar difficulties; expectations, whether too high or too low; the state; the school; the church and its dogma; "the tyranny of tradition;" politics and political rivalries; drugs; addiction and addictive personalities; habits, instincts, and impulses; genetics; biology; psychology; and when all else fails, God (or the Devil, whichever is most useful in the moment). Marxism, modernism, post-modernism- all these masks of materialism- have begun brought into question the very mechanism by which man overcomes himself and his disadvantages. Society has begun to *unravel;* it will *continue to unravel.*

The modern problem is that liberalism as we now know it has- perhaps unwittingly- become a euphemism for the *internalization of slave-psychology,* and therefore as a natural consequence, for the *externalization of slave-psychology as well.* It runs contrary to the flourishing of the human being because it negates freedom of will in practice, which is the sole means through which the human being is capable of realizing himself *as human*. For the question of whether or not free will exists is a logical complement to the question of whether or not we are to be *victors* or *victims,* whether or not we are even *capable* of choosing liberty or slavery. Progressives all agree that slavery is dehumanizing, and yet they cannot help but to perpetuate an ideology that leads their fellow man directly into *mental* slavery, which can only result in his eventual *material* slavery as well. Because when things go bad (as they inevitably do), the unfree identity will beg for the chain, clamoring for more and more social control in order to feel safe and secure. Generally speaking, of course, progressives have little idea that they are promoting a contradiction. The liberal overseers know it but do not care; the liberal underlings do not know it but have been brainwashed into a state of near-perpetual cognitive dissonance, so they never reflect upon their own ideological inconsistencies- what was referred to in the dystopian classic *1984* as *doublethink.*

What is most critical to the flourishing of the human being and therefore to the flourishing of human society in general is that the individual be *healthy, of strong will, and morally responsible for himself.* When these conditions have not been obtained, or worse, when they have been obstructed and then systematically abolished, then the fundamental ground upon which society is dependent is brought into question. Just as the chain is only so strong as its weakest link, so the nation is only so strong as its weakest man. For the quality of a culture, government, society is directed determined by the quality *of its citizens.*

When the locus of power is reoriented from *internal* to *external*- that is, when it is moved from the individual to something other and alien to the individual-, conditions become ripe for tyranny. Given the choice between order and chaos, the vast majority of individuals will choose order, even if that order comes at the cost of their own freedom. Human beings require, like all other animals, *regularity* in order to survive and to thrive in a dangerous world; they need to be able to reasonably predict not only *the world itself,* but also *the behavior of other animals in the world.* Yet a chaotic system cannot be predicted, and so evolution has carved out numberless drives, programs, and subroutines dedicated to the recognition of consistent systems of order. We need these; if necessary, we will trade *anything* for them.

The practical consequence of post-modern social engineering is "the modern mind," one in which *internal order* is lacking, one that accepts *external order* and *external order alone* as the remedy. But human beings possess more *potential* than any other animal; thus, human beings also require more *discipline* than any other animal, for we have the capacity to choose anything at all- *including our own destruction.* This is not so much the case for the rest of the animal kingdom, where hard-wired instincts are far more dominant and where the animal possesses far less freedom of self-determination, but it is certainly the case with us. So by thwarting the development of self-determination in the individual, post-modernism has reversed the natural order of things. Predictably, this has been to disastrous effect.

It is this *otherness of agency,* this pathological need *to project personal responsibility upon the external world,* that most obviously defines post-modernism. The gift of freedom is a double-edged sword: It may entail grave danger, and the progressive response to that danger is the abdication of the very quality that makes us human. Socially, the consequences of this pattern of response are catastrophic, for it results in two diametric conditions that virtually ensure tyranny: inflation of the ego to ridiculous proportions as a psychological counterbalance to its lack of self-determination, and thus the latent wish to rule over absolutely everything; and base abjection before some powerful individual or group of individuals stemming from the previously discussed need for order, which, paradoxically, is generally accompanied by an enormous amount of resentment and vengefulness directed towards said powerful individual or group of individuals. These two drives are contradictory, and result in a society that looks forward to the coming of a master strong enough to set things right while also simultaneously looking forward to that moment when the slaves will be free to run wild.

The basic problem with Marxist philosophies, therefore, is that they create a psychology in which the Marxist both *loves* and *hates* the powerful, specifically because he learns to misunderstand where freedom really comes from; he mistakenly externalizes the source of his own liberation. *There is nothing external to the self can ever really be controlled.* And yet for the progressive- because he is lacking in control over himself-, compensation *in the external world* for a lack of control *of the internal world* is the only solution, hence his obsession with power structures. This animosity towards the powerful is really a displaced awareness that something *is very, very wrong,* and it has serious social repurcussions. Sadly, self-reflection is rare once the rightful order of things has been sent all topsy-turvy; once the will has been destroyed, there is very often no going back.

We have only to scan the language of the progressive in order to see exactly what it is that he *really* believes: It is language that utterly demonizes power of any kind *even while kneeling before it.* And that language *polarizes* society, dividing complex human beings into overly-simplistic categories: male/female, white/black, *bourgeoisie*/proletariat, and so forth. This is done in order to dehumanize the enemy, which is merely anybody who seems to possess more power than the progressive feels that he himself possesses. But because this method of division is entirely subjective, there is no operation by which the problem can be solved- though of course that is how the overseers like it…

In the beginning, overseers will keep the underlings in the dark; at the conclusion, underlings will refuse to be enlightened even if offered. This is because the underling has been educated (indoctrinated) to view truth is a kind of *violation.* [Illumination is, after all, a kind of *forcing into consciousness;* it is *the forceful shattering of delusion,* which identity experiences as a threat.] Thus, the underling is in his quintessence utterly *fragile;* he is always ready *to fracture.* But if he is indeed powerless, then *he* cannot put the world aright; *another* is required to put the world aright- *a mouthpiece of slaves.* And this may be the best reason for why modern politics has become such a fiasco: The political arena has become a kind of *Circus Maximus* where the most powerful weapon of any contender is not ability at all but rather the entertainment of the mob.

However, because the drive for power still exists at the root of post-modernism, when the mouthpiece of slaves- that is, "the representative of the people's freedom"- finally acquires it, he is almost immediately be corrupted by it. Because the mouthpiece of slaves *is himself enslaved* and thus possesses no more self-mastery than those that he speaks for. But there is no worse steward of power than a slave, and the most vicious dictators and the most blood-soaked political revolutionaries in recent history have all risen to positions of authority in the name of the people: Benito Mussolini, Adolph Hitler, Joseph Stalin, Mao Zedong, Pol Pot, Che Guevara, Kim Jong-Il- all became powerful through populism following a period of cultural crisis, no matter their position on the political spectrum. This destablization of society results in a radical need for order at any cost- and in the mind of the revolutionary justifies any atrocity: the Reign of Terror, the Holocaust, the Khmer Rouge, etc.

The connection between populism and revolution is no accident; the psychology of the revolutionary is similar throughout history. For instance, Maximilien Robespierre, the father of the French Revolution, wrote in 1794, "If the basis of popular governent in peacetime is virtue, the basis of popular government during a revolution is both virtue and terror: virtue, without which terror is baneful; terror, without which virtue is powerless." Vladimir Lenin, who orchestrated the Red Terror, echoed his sentiments, "We need the real, nation-wide terror that reinvigorates the country and through which the Great French Revolution achieved glory." Revolutionaries, it would seem, are nothing if not consistent.

Thus the absence of self-mastery necessarily results in the entire *culture of enslavement*- both the slave *and* the slave-master. And so it is a very short step indeed from post-modernism to political tyranny- not to mention cultural self-destruction. After all, suicidality is nothing if not resignation before the fear that *all is hopeless,* that in all the world, *nothing at all matters.* Because this results in the very nightmare prophesied by the madman of *Thus Spake Zarathustra,* a time in which man has lost all hope, a time in which what is brightest and strongest within him has been finally snuffed out, a time in which the godly within him has been destroyed, never to be resurrected.

This cannot be allowed.

Post-modernism will destroy the world as we know it; it is *already* destroying the world as we know it. Whatever is strong and healthy and virtuous, whatever is capable of securing a future for mankind, has been endangered by post-modernism and its ten thousand puppet ideologies, which multiply like the heads of the Hydra. The true future of humanity is ensured by freedom of will constrained by respect for truth; modern liberal philosophy destroys the will. And it destroys the individual and all his potential and possibility along with it.

Post-modernism and self-destruction belong together. They share a singular psychological core: *akrasia,* weakness of will; luckily, they also share a singular psychological cure: *enkrateia,* power over the self. Therefore, if one truly wishes to set the world aright, then he must first reflect deeply upon the problem, seek out its causes and conditions, and do what must be done in order to rectify the situation. Because the goal must always be to strike at the heart of the disease; thus far, our would-be physicians have only been concerned with symptoms and superficialities.

In conclusion, the spiritual poisoning of generation after generation of otherwise right-thinking human beings must be abandoned. And our childish utopian obsession with a perfect world- whatever that means- must likewise be abandoned. After all, liberation from *slavery of the self-* the *truest* slavery of all- is impossible without the destruction of its ideological epicenter, which is the absurd assertion that willpower is a fantasy, and that self-determination is a problem to be solved. *That* is the enemy; *that* is the corruption of the human being, and it can only result in tyranny.

All is not hopeless. Self-mastery brings freedom; freedom brings fulfillment and the flourishing of humanity. Fortunately, the path to self-mastery is open to each of us at any time, in any place because it lies within. Fulfillment and the flourshing of humanity follow necessarily. So we must stick to the path. For on that path, anything is possible; on that path, we can set the world aright.

ABOUT THE AUTHOR

Joshua van Asakinda was born 22 September, 1979 near Pittsburgh, Pennsylvania. He holds a master's degree in psychology from American Military University and a bachelor's degree in psychology and philosophy from the University of Pittsburgh. For years, he went traveling in search of himself; this led him to the Mahayana, and to the establishment of various protocols fusing religion, martial studies, and evolutionary psychology. Now he has self-published a number of books, including *Slay the Maiden; Profiling the Left; Stranging the Beautiful Noise; Strategies of Guerrilla Psychology I: Valhalla;* and *Strategies of Guerrilla Psychology II: ZenTactics.* Finally, he is Chan Buddhist, First of the Zenshida'i, creator of *Pencak Silat Cimande dari Zenshida'i.*